IMAGES
of America

NORTH BRANFORD
AND
NORTHFORD
1850–1950

The Reynolds-Beers House, built in 1786 by Hezekiah Reynolds, was the town clerk's office from 1920 to 1960, when Ralph Beers, and later his wife, Ruth Judson Beers, served in that capacity. The house, located next to the Atwater Library, was purchased by the Town in August 1997 and is used by the Totoket Historical Society as a museum and learning center for local history. (THS.)

IMAGES
of America

NORTH BRANFORD
AND
NORTHFORD
1850–1950

Janet S. Gregan and Grace Rapone Marx
for the Totoket Historical Society, Inc.

ARCADIA

First published 1998
Copyright © The Totoket Historical Society, 1998

ISBN 0-7524-0952-0

Published by Arcadia Publishing,
an imprint of the Chalford Publishing Corporation,
One Washington Center, Dover, New Hampshire 03820.
Printed in Great Britain

Library of Congress Cataloging-in-Publication Data applied for

Prior to 1940 quiet, tree-lined, narrow, dirt roads similar to this view of Cedar Lake Road, earlier known as Smith's road, were typical of the town roads in North Branford. (THS.)

Contents

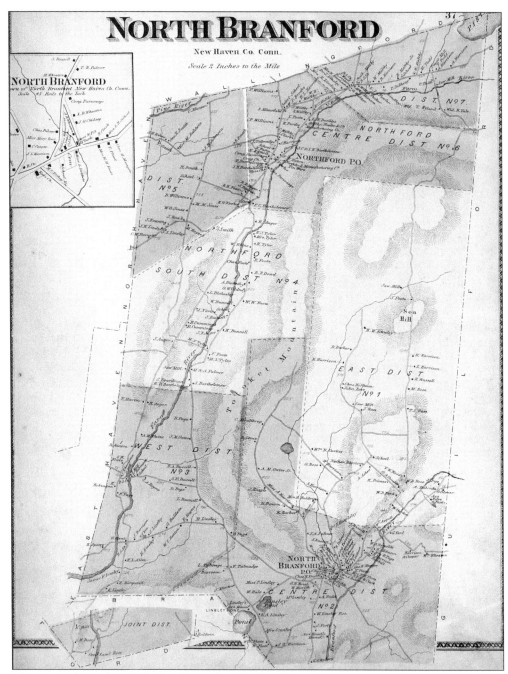

This map of North Branford and Northford, taken from the 1868 *Beers Atlas of New Haven County*, shows the town's two villages, seven school districts, topography of the land, location of the churches, mills, and manufactories, and the homes and names of the residents. This was mapped long before the New Haven Water Company acquired one-third of the town in 1925 and built the dam that created Lake Gaillard. (THS.)

Introduction

Until the mid-twentieth century, North Branford was a small country town. First settled in 1695 as the north farms of Branford, the Second and North Society of Branford (North Branford) and the Third Society (Northford) separated from their parent town and joined together to establish the town of North Branford in 1831. The two villages, each with its own churches, stores, and schools, remained the distinct entities they are today.

The whole town had a population of about one thousand people from the Revolutionary War years until the early twentieth century. The population doubled by 1950 and then began rapidly to increase as the old farms were sold and subdivided into building lots. Today, with a population of approximately fourteen thousand, North Branford is a suburban community.

As we approach the twenty-first century, the rural aspect of North Branford is swiftly disappearing (even though one-third of the town's geographic area is owned by the South Central Connecticut Regional Water Authority and remains open space). Out of the hundreds of small farms that existed in 1850, only a handful remain today. The small-town feeling of one hundred years ago, when everyone knew everyone (or at least knew of them), has disappeared along with the openness of the landscape and the slow quiet pace of everyday life.

The Totoket Historical Society, Inc. (THS) was created forty years ago in 1958 by a group of people concerned that the past would be forgotten if something wasn't done to preserve it. They began by collecting items and documents pertaining to the history of the town. Various individuals began researching and recording different aspects of that history and much of the research was used in Dr. Herbert C. Miller's *History of North Branford and Branford*, published by the Totoket Historical Society in 1980. The collection has grown from a few items housed in a metal cabinet at the Smith Library to thousands of documents and implements stored in the vaults at the THS Center. Among the items donated over the years were many wonderful old photographs.

This book is part of the continuing effort of the Totoket Historical Society to share its knowledge about the town's history with residents, students, and other interested people. It is an attempt to portray the way we were from 1850 to 1950, when North Branford truly was a small rural town.

Janet S. Gregan and Grace Rapone Marx
October 1997

Acknowledgments

Most of the photographs used in this publication are from the collection of the Totoket Historical Society, Inc. The society thanks the following people and organizations who lent their treasured photographs to supplement our collection: Marion Bradley, Margaret Cremin, Marie Frione, Henry Forte, Dudley Harrison, Gertrude Heath, Grace Marx, Dorothy Neubig, Ann Neubig, the North Branford Congregational Church, Bertha Page, Ellen Spencer, Susan Shea, St. Andrew's Episcopal Church, St. Augustine's Catholic Church, Barbara Stone, Evelyn Surprenant, Mary Wallace, Leta Wharton, and the Zion Church.

The society also thanks the following people for the recent donations of photographs to the Totoket Historical Society, Inc., some of which were used: Marjorie Boyce Patten, for the photographs taken by her father, Paul Boyce; Elsie Loeber Jones; Florence Scholz Hogan; Clarence Hyland; James McKeown; Evelyn Surprenant; Edward Wall; and the South Central Connecticut Regional Water Authority. The society is grateful for earlier donations of photographs from Florence Juniver, Gordon Miller, and Randy Simpson.

The authors thank James Shea for legal services and James McKeown and Eugene MacMullan for proofreading. We also thank the Board of Directors of the Totoket Historical Society, Inc., for their support.

We, the authors, would like to add that we know there may be some areas that are not covered in this visual history of North Branford and Northford. We were limited by the photographs available for this book.

J.S.G. and G.R.M.

One
The North Farms

North Branford began as the north farms of Branford when the sons and grandsons of the first settlers came to build their homesteads and carve their farms out of a wilderness. They built their farms by the two ponds now known as Cedar and Linsley Lakes, at Bare Plains, in the valley between the hilltop ridges that now contains Lake Gaillard, and along the Branford and Farm Rivers. They farmed up until the mid-twentieth century just the way their fathers and grandfathers did. Here are a few of the farms of North Branford and Northford.

These cows belonged to Gus Loeber, whose farm was located at the intersection of what is now Route 80 and Notch Hill Road. Keenan's Funeral Home now stands in the spot where the cows are drinking from a small pond. (THS.)

The Linsley Farm was located on Twin Lakes Road between the two "ponds." Only the house remains today. This view, taken from the hill on the corner of Cedar Lake Road on June 21, 1935, shows Charles Linsley cutting hay. (THS.)

In this view of their farm on the same June day in 1935, the men of two Linsley families work together to harvest the hay. George operates the hayrake, and John pitches the loose hay to Ernest, who stacks it on the hay wagon. The hay field was located just to the south of Cedar Lake Road. (THS.)

Salvatore Rapone guides Jerry, the horse, while Roland Hall handles the plow as they prepare the ground for a victory garden at their two-family home at the Rivaldi-owned farm on Twin Lakes Road about 1944. (THS.)

This view of the Rivaldi Farm shows the two stucco houses (only one stands today) on Twin Lakes Road and the hill where Summit Drive is now located. The owner, Peter Rivaldi (standing), chats with an unidentified friend in this photograph taken about 1940. (THS.)

The acreage belonging to the large, thriving Shapiro Farm, originally owned by William I. Benton on the Foxon Turnpike (now Route 80), is today the site of the Doral Farms subdivision. The Shapiros operated one of the first vegetable stands in town during the 1920s and 1930s. (Susan Shea.)

Across the road from Shapiro's land stood the Dudley Farm. The house is now used for a nursery school, and the open farmlands are the area where the North Branford Intermediate School, North Branford High School, the Ray Reigeluth tennis courts, and the high school athletic fields are located. (Susan Shea.)

The Page Farm on Totoket Road has been in the same family since the town was first settled. Today the dairy farm is operated by Bob Page and his family. This photograph taken about 1908 shows the house where the family still lives and the barn that burnt in 1957. The building in the foreground was called the milk house. (Bertha Page.)

Dick Page operates the harrow on his farm, while an unidentified farmhand does the seeding in a spring photograph taken about 1925. For many years the Page family operated the Maple Shade Dairy, delivering milk to the schools and selling it out of a small building on the farm now used to house the McGlynn Construction Company. (Bertha Page.)

Men of the Augur family proudly show off their horses in this *c.* 1935 photograph. From left to right are brothers Joseph, George, Fred, and Elbert. (Margaret Cremin.)

The Augur Farm stood on Totoket Road in Northford near the intersection of Parsonage Hill Road to the west and Augur Road to the east. At the time this photograph was taken, about 1940, it was a full-scale farming operation. Some of the barns are still standing today. (Dorothy Neubig.)

Ida Augur feeds the turkeys at the turkey farm operated by her and her sister Laura. It was part of the Augur Farm complex in Northford. This photograph was taken about 1935. (Ann Neubig.)

At his Grassy Hill Turkey Farm on Maple Road in North Branford, Edward Wall Sr. feeds his turkeys in a photograph taken about 1949. (Edward Wall Jr.)

Haying on the Forest Road Trieschmann Farm was a family affair in the 1920s. Here Maria stands on the hay wagon while her husband, Martin, stands to the right and Martin Jr. pitches hay. (Gertrude Trieschmann Heath.)

The Trieschmann Farm is located on the Totoket ridge side of Forest Road (Route 22) between Old Forest Road and Augur Road in Northford. This photograph showing the dirt road and farm complex was taken March 24, 1935. Earlier, in the mid-nineteenth century, the farm was owned by the Tyler family. (Gertrude Heath.)

During the early part of the twentieth century, there were many fruit farms and orchards in North Branford, and some of the farmers were well known for their fine strawberries. This 1932 photograph shows the strawberry fields at the Harrison Farm on North Street. The stand in the foreground was where the pickers would have their baskets counted. (Dudley Harrison.)

Corn and field crops were important to North Branford farmers, and there are still many corn fields around town today. Here 6-foot-tall William and Daniel Doody are dwarfed by an especially high stand of corn grown in 1925 on their family farm along Route 80. (Marion Doody Bradley.)

Henry Forte sits on his horse at his family farm on Mill Road for this photograph taken about 1945. (Henry Forte.)

In 1929, Cavaliere Forte purchased the old Page Farm on Mill Road and with the help of his sons, Jack, Henry, and Charles, ran a large dairy farm. The family also operated a slaughterhouse on Route 80 and was well known all over the East Coast for their milk-fed veal. (Henry Forte.)

Henry Forte and one of his brothers milk cows in the large barn on their Mill Road farm, a chore that had to be done twice a day. When milk prices dropped in 1956 and it was no longer profitable to run a dairy farm, the Fortes sold their herd, and part of the farm became one of the town's first subdivisions, North Branford Estates. (Henry Forte.)

Agnes and William Lelasher feed a pig at their small farm on Middletown Avenue in Northford about 1940. It was not uncommon for families to raise a pig or two for their own consumption, especially during the Great Depression of the 1930s and the World War II years. (Ellen Spencer.)

Five-year-old Clifford Harrison stands in front of the sap house at the old Harrison Farm in North Branford about 1912. Since its settlement, North Branford farmers have tapped the abundant maple trees on their farms in the early spring to gather sap and make maple syrup and sugar. The Harrison family still makes and sells maple syrup today on North Street. (Dudley Harrison.)

In 1939, the Harrisons collected the sap from the buckets on each tree and poured it into large milk cans to be transported by truck to the sap house, where it would be boiled down to make maple syrup and sugar. In early years the sap would be transported by horse and wagon, or if there was snow on the ground, by horse and sledge. (Dudley Harrison.)

The Shagbark Dairy Farm was owned and operated by John King on Eight Mile Hill in Northford, on the road that is now Old Turnpike. This photograph taken in 1940 shows the openness of the farm fields with the Totoket ridgeline in the background. (Barbara Stone.)

Water for farming operations had to be pumped by hand. Here Peter Rivaldi and Dante Marchetti pump a bucket full on the Rivaldi Farm on Twin Lakes Road about 1935. (THS.)

A placid winter farm scene shows the home and farm of Elbert and Margaret Augur on Middletown Avenue, Northford, in a photograph taken in 1934. (Mary Wallace.)

This photograph, taken on June 30, 1935, shows John, Mary, Amy, and Clara Linsley herding the cows home for milking. The animals had spent the day grazing in a pasture belonging to the Linsley Farm on Twin Lakes Road. (THS.)

Two

The Families and Their Homesteads

The first families who came to North Branford and Northford were descendants of the Puritans who had settled in Branford and surrounding towns. They had names like Harrison, Linsley, Augur, Page, Baldwin, Russell, Williams, Smith, and Bunnell. In the nineteenth century, people from countries other than England began to arrive, first to work on the farms as laborers and later to buy the farms and marry into the local families. They had names like Hoffman, Walsh, and Doody. The industries in the twentieth century brought more families to town, mostly from Italy and eastern Europe. By 1950, the people of North Branford and Northford were a mix of nationalities, which has become even more diverse today. Illustrated are a few examples of the homes and the families who lived in town before 1950.

The 1872 William M. Fowler house still stands on its original site on Middletown Avenue, Northford. In the summer of 1889, the Linsly family was living here and posed for this photograph. From left to right are J.J. Linsly; his wife, Caroline Maltby Linsly; and their children, Eunice Hall, Jared, and Maud Maltby. (THS.)

The old Augur homestead that stood on Totoket Road in Northford was taken down in 1963. Here the family of George and Cecelia Dumont Augur and the first ten of their thirteen children line up for a family portrait about 1912. They are, from left to right, Ethel, Helen, Irene, Charles, Esther, Grace, Elbert, Fred, George, and Joe. (Dorothy Neubig.)

Donald and Laura Augur feed their pet sheep at the Augur Farm about 1922. Laura and Donald were the last two children of George and Cecelia Augur. (Margaret Cremin.)

Charles Alling stands by his mail wagon in front of the Linsly-Alling house on Old Post Road about 1910. He delivered mail to Northford residents. The house was built by Josiah Linsly for his son, Eliakim, in 1820 and still stands today. (THS.)

Miss Edna Davis poses on the porch of her family home in a photograph probably taken about 1900. This house stood facing Middletown Avenue across from the Northford Company #2 Firehouse. Her father was postmaster of the Northford Post Office, and for several years the Northford Post Office, established in 1802, was located here. (THS.)

The house on the corner of Middletown Avenue and Maltby Lane in Northford was built for Samuel Maltby about 1838, and his descendants occupied it until 1930. The girl on the right is Mary Alling Miller. This house is a good example of the Greek Revival style; many existing houses in town were built in this style between 1820 and 1860. (THS.)

A family poses with their new automobile in front of a house identified as the Old Rose House on North Street. This house is a later version of the Greek Revival style. It is now gone, as it was one of the houses that was taken down in 1926, when the New Haven Water Company built the dam for their reservoir at Lake Gaillard. (NBCC.)

This was the residence of William Merrick, a descendent of North Branford's first minister, Jonathan Merrick. It was built in the mid-nineteenth century, replacing Jonathan's 1727 house, and stood where Central Shopping Plaza is now located. Early this century it was owned by James Walsh, and it was here, in one of the upper rooms, that the first Catholic Mass was held in town on February 29, 1920. (THS.)

One of the oldest houses in North Branford stands on Cedar Lake Road. It was probably built about 1704 by Samuel Pond. It was acquired by Daniel Linsley in 1774 and stayed in the Linsley family until it was purchased by Frank Smith in 1881. His family lived here until the mid-twentieth century. (THS.)

Jerome Harrison is a well-known name in town. His nephew, Jonathan Merrick, donated part of the land he inherited from his uncle to the Town to build the Jerome Harrison School. Jerome himself gave the portion of his land where he had laid his only child, Amoret, to rest when she died at the age of seventeen in 1860 for use as the Bare Plains Cemetery. (Evelyn Surprenant.)

Jerome Harrison lived in the house where his father, Col. Thaddeus Harrison, kept a tavern. It was built about 1805, and the front gable was probably added about 1880. The house still stands on Route 80. (Evelyn Surprenant.)

Dr. Clara Smith was the daughter of Edward and Georgianna Smith. Her father was a partner in the firm, Smith and Cowles Co. in Northford, that in 1861 patented and manufactured a self-operated horse-drawn hayrake. Clara, who attended Yale College, was a professor and the head of the mathematics department at Wellsley College. (THS.)

The Smith family lived in this Gothic Revival cottage that still stands on Maltby Lane. Clara Smith used the family home as a summer place. She left the house and the rest of her estate to the Town to build a library in memory of her father. The Edward Smith Memorial Library was built in 1957. (THS.)

Frank Davis and an unidentified friend take a break from their farm chores about 1915. According to one source, Frank was involved in buying and selling calves and bringing them to a New Haven slaughterhouse. (THS.)

The Davis family lived in this house on Middletown Avenue built about 1839 by George Fowler. George was one of six sons of Maltby Fowler, who came to Northford from Milford in 1820 and established a wagon factory. The family invented many different machines to produce a variety of items from screws to perforated tinware. George invented a machine for making tin lamps and another for making platinum rivets. (THS.)

Three generations of Augur women posed for this shot taken near the old family homestead on Totoket Road. They are Cecelia Dumont Augur, Esther Augur Doody (her daughter), and Cecelia's granddaughter Cecelia, always called Ceil. Esther Doody lived all her married life in the old Edward Linsley house on Route 80, where she had a chicken farm and was well known for selling chickens and eggs. (Dorothy Neubig.)

Two friends, Catherine Battista (left) and Angelina Amatrudo, mug for the camera after church on Sunday about 1920. They are in front of the Camarota family home that stood on the north side of Route 80 just 20 feet away from the railroad tracks. The house, which belonged to David Page in 1868, is gone and the property is now part of the Trap Rock Quarry operation. (THS.)

May Page, daughter of Rev. Charles and Elbertine A. (Dudley) Page, married Jonathan Merrick in 1892. Both the bride and groom were descendants of the first settlers in North Branford, and some of their descendants still reside in town today. (Evelyn Surprenant.)

On April 6, 1926, Louise Camarota married Fiori Rapone, the first marriage to take place in the newly built St. Augustine Catholic Church on Branford Road. The Camarotas moved to North Branford in 1914, when the New Haven Trap Rock Quarry was established. Fiori and his brother Salvatore came to town about 1920 to work at the quarry. (Marie Frione.)

The dining room of the Augustus Rogers house on Mill Road was decorated for a family occasion sometime in the mid-nineteenth century. (Leta Wharton.)

The Augustus Rogers house was built in the 1700s by Thomas Rogers. Augustus was Thomas's grandson and the great-grandson of Abijah, who owned the mill at Page's Pond. Augustus left the house to his adopted son, Rev. Charles Page, who built a new house next door in 1876 (where Henry Forte now lives). The old house was eventually taken down. (Leta Wharton.)

33

From left to right, the Merrick children—Lucius, Elbertine, Velma, and Leta—pose with their toys outside the play house made for them by their father, Jonathan Merrick, on the family property that was located on what is now the corner of Merrick Drive and Route 80. The ornate door was the headboard from a bed. (Leta Wharton.)

Frederick Harrison pulls his three-year-old brother Clifford and his animal friends in a homemade wagon. The snapshot was taken about 1910. (Dudley Harrison.)

Anita Rapone and Jimmy Iovieno pose for this 1946 snapshot in the front yard of the home of Anita's grandparents, Nicholas and Frances Buccelli, on Twin Lakes Road. The house was built about 1845 for Frederick W. Beers, whose grandfather, Wheeler Beers, built the first house in this area in the mid-eighteenth century. The house is now a multi-family dwelling. (Grace Marx.)

Bernard Amatrudo stands by the driveway of his parent's gas station on Route 80 in a snapshot taken about 1940. In the background is the home of his grandparents, Bernard and Clare Lanzo. The house is gone and Twin Lakes Commons is now located here. (Linda Cantore.)

This formal family portrait shows Frances (Mrs. Joseph) Camarota and her four children: Mary, Bella, Louise, and Sam. In 1914 the Camarota family became one of the first families to move to town because of work at the New Haven Trap Rock Quarry. Descendants with the names Rapone, Camarota, Davis, DaCunto, Wysocki, Lennon, Frione, Carafola, and Marx continue to live in North Branford today. (Marie Frione.)

Seated on the steps of 1790 Josiah Linsley house on Old Post Road, Northford, are Charles Simpson, Agnes Linsley, Charlotte E. Maltby, Eunice Simpson, and Mr. and Mrs. Evart Stevens. The children are Charles and Herbert Miller and Charles Alling. Eunice Simpson was the president of the Northford Historical Institute, which later became the Totoket Historical Society, Inc. Dr. Herbert C. Miller wrote *The History of North Branford and Northford* in 1980. (THS.)

On April 3, 1921, the Doody brothers—William (left), John (center), and Daniel—stood on the steps of the George Baldwin house for this snapshot. This house, attributed to architect Ithiel Town, stands on Route 80 and looks like a small Greek temple. Micah Baldwin, a New York merchant, built it for his nephew George in 1842. It is listed in the National Register of Historic Places. (Marion Bradley.)

A few years earlier, in 1919, the Hart family was living in the George Baldwin house and posed for a picture at the same spot. John Bernard Hart and his wife, Frances Carrier Hart, are surrounded by their children, Marie, Helen (in her father's lap), John Jr., and twins Jim and Leslie. (Ellen Spencer.)

Martha Russell (1817–1899) was an author of some renown. As early as 1840 she was writing articles for the *National Era* in Washington, D.C. She later wrote for the *Knickerbocker* and *Columbian* magazines, had three novels published, and wrote poetry. A descendent of Samuel Russell, the minister when North Branford was settled, she lived in the family homestead on Sea Hill Road (now gone), where McMahon Drive is now located. (THS.)

Rev. Charles Page was born in North Branford in 1839, the son of Benjamin and Sarah Merriam Page. He was the town clerk from 1871 to 1920, a school visitor, and also served three terms as the Republican senator from the 6th District, during which he was chairman of the "important Committee on Temperance." A schoolteacher, he attended Yale Divinity School and became pastor of the Foxon Congregational Church in 1894. (Evelyn Surprenant.)

Jennette Linsly Maltby (Mrs. Charles) Alling (1850–1913) was the mother of Rev. Morris Alling, who with his wife, Jean Cooke Alling, purchased the "Sol's Path House" in 1928, bringing it back into the family after fifty years. They restored it under the guidance of noted architectural historian J. Frederick Kelly. Jean Cooke Alling wrote about the house in her book, *A Silent Witness in Four Centuries*. (THS.)

The house on Sol's Path, a private road off Middletown Avenue, was built about 1705 by Benjamin Howd, a carpenter. In 1740, he sold it to Joseph Linsly, and the house remained in the Linsly family until 1875. Sol's Path was named for Joseph's son, Solomon (1751–1814). This house is listed in the National Register of Historic Places. (THS.)

Dudley Harrison, son of Clifford and Lucy (Dudley) Harrison, wanders down Sea Hill Road by the George T. Fowler house, built about 1926. The home was built on the site of an older house and today is a multi-family dwelling. (Dudley Harrison.)

Schoolboy Bruno Belbusti lingers along Mill Road near the Totoket schoolhouse about 1920. This bucolic scene with its dirt road and open fields is representative of what the town was like before the population explosion of the mid-twentieth century. Now, North Branford Estates, a housing development, is located next to the old schoolhouse. (THS.)

Three

The Churches and Meetinghouses

The four churches in town were the main focal point of community life until the mid-twentieth century. The original two meetinghouses that served the Second and Third Societies are long gone, replaced before 1850 with newer buildings for their congregational members. There was also an Episcopal church at each end of town, St. Andrew's in Northford and the Zion in North Branford. The first Roman Catholic church, St. Augustine's, was built in 1925. By 1950, the Catholic population was expanding rapidly, and two years later St. Monica's was built in Northford. In 1962, the new St. Augustine's was erected on Caputo Road. There are now other churches of other faiths in North Branford and all continue to serve as focal points for much of today's community activities.

The second meetinghouse of the North Branford Congregational Church was built in 1831, replacing the first meetinghouse that had been built in 1724 in this location "on the knoll near the river by Samuel Harrison's." The main road seen in this photograph taken about 1900 is Route 80; the narrower dirt path that forks off to the left is Church Street. (THS.)

The Congregational church was built just in time for the first town meeting to be held in its basement when the town of North Branford was established in May 1831. This photograph taken about 1905 shows the Civil War Monument that was erected in 1866, reputed to be one of the first such monuments in the country. (THS.)

Sunday school students line up on the front steps of the North Branford Congregational Church in 1892. This picture belonged to Grace and Bertha Foote, and it can be assumed that they are in the photograph. (THS.)

A postcard view of the 1831 North Branford Congregational Church and Chapel shows the horse sheds and the Philo Harrison house in the rear. The chapel was built in 1887 using funds raised by the women so that the Ladies Sewing Society, established in 1878, would have a place to meet. The General Philo Harrison house was built in 1820 as a tavern. (THS.)

A disastrous fire in 1908 left the North Branford Congregational Church in rubble. The chapel was spared when town residents formed a bucket brigade to the Branford River, keeping the roof wet. In the background is the 1784 Jacob Page house. Jacob served in the Revolutionary War, was taken prisoner by the British, and was imprisoned in England. He sold the house to Nathan Harrison in 1809 and moved away. (THS.)

The citizens of the town pledged support to build a new church, and the present North Branford Congregational Church was rebuilt immediately on the foundation of the second meetinghouse. The style of the church was chosen at an Ecclesiastical Society meeting where the women of the church were allowed to vote for the first time ever. (THS.)

The interior view of the new church building shows the choir area and organ behind the railing, and the central pulpit with the communion table below it. (NBCC.)

The North Branford Congregational Church Parsonage on North Street was acquired in 1838 and used until 1957. It was originally built in 1772 for Daniel and Sarah (Frisbie) Rose. The third minister of the church, Charles Atwater, purchased it in 1809 and lived here until he died of typhoid fever in 1825. The house is now a private dwelling. (NBCC.)

This view of the North Branford Congregational Church shows it in the winter about 1925. Compare this with the photograph on p. 41. The elms that lined the old Foxon-Killingworth Turnpike are long gone, but the Civil War Soldiers monument, the sign post, the flagpole (now replaced with a newer version), and the old store are still in existence. (THS.)

The Northford Congregational Church, designed by Henry Austin and built in 1845, burned in 1906 and was rebuilt using much of the original stone work. It still stands today on the location of the original 1745 Meeting House at the corner of Old Post Road and Clintonville Road. This picture was probably taken about 1941. (THS—Paul Boyce Collection.)

Sunday school students, dressed for some special occasion, and their parents pose on the steps of the Northford Congregational Church in 1923. Somewhere in the group is John Miller and his mother, Mary Miller. (THS.)

The Northford Congregational Parsonage stood across Old Post Road from the church. The eighteenth-century residence served as a parsonage from 1836 until it burned in 1944. The current parsonage was erected on the same site soon after. (THS.)

The Northford Congregational Church Parsonage burnt down on May 29, 1944, and was replaced with the present parsonage. This fire was instrumental in creating a volunteer fire department in Northford, which was formed as the North Branford Volunteer Fire Department, Company #2. (THS.)

This *c.* 1890 photograph was taken on the steps of the Northford Congregational Church. No one now living has been able to explain on what occasion the photograph was taken. However, there is an undocumented story that Northford residents had been hit by a plague or widespread

sickness around this time, and that many had died. Those who survived may have dressed in their best and posed for this formal portrait in celebration of being spared. The story may be true because many of the people portrayed here were not members of the church. (THS.)

St. Andrew's Episcopal Church, located high on a hill on Middletown Avenue in the center of Northford, was built in 1845 and later burned in 1938. The first Episcopal church in town was established in 1763 and stood on the spot that is now the parking lot for the William Douglas Commons. (THS.)

This shot of the interior of St. Andrew's Episcopal Church was taken about 1900 before electricity had come to Northford. When this church was built in 1845, the parish of St. Andrew's had thirty-two families, forty-nine communicants, and a Sunday school with three teachers and twenty pupils. (St. Andrew's.)

The St. Andrew's choir poses on Old Home Day, October 6, 1935. Pictured, from left to right, are the following: (front row) Martha Andersen (third from left), Delma Williams, Hazel Salg, Joseph Salg, Gertrude Williams, Roger Williams, unidentified, Isabella Lockwood, Evelyn Alta, and Muriel Williams; (back row) Carl Harrison, Leander Williams, unidentified, Rev. Francis J. Smith, unidentified, Gertrude Salg, three unidentified persons, Donald Williams, two unidentified persons, and Gerald Smith. (St. Andrew's.)

After the 1938 fire, groundbreaking for the new St. Andrew's Episcopal Church was held October 1, 1939, on a cold, rainy day. Pictured in the center is Rev. Francis J. Smith. (THS.)

The Warham Williams House that stood in the center of Northford next to the Northford Store was used as the Episcopal rectory from 1866 to 1942. Originally built in 1752 by the first minister of the Northford Congregational Church, Warham Williams, it was occupied by Rev. Matthew Noyes from 1791 to 1835 and then was a private home. The building was dismantled in 1977 and moved to Roxbury, Connecticut. (THS.)

After the 1938 St. Andrew's Episcopal Church fire, the Warham Williams house was used for worship services until the new church was built. This photograph shows how it looked during Sunday services at that time. (St. Andrew's.)

The new St. Andrew's Church, built on the same spot, was modeled after the 1845 building with a square bell tower and simple Gothic interior. The houses in the background are the 1855 Isaac Bartholomew house and the 1780 Timothy Bartholomew house at the corner of Clintonville Road (both are still standing). In the mid-nineteenth century, the Northford Post Office was located in the older house. (St. Andrew's.)

The consecration of the new St. Andrew's Episcopal Church was held on November 10, 1940. (St. Andrew's.)

The Zion Episcopal Church, built in 1818, stood on Route 80 between the cemetery and the 1979 North Branford Town Hall. It was built by Capt. Abraham Coan, who also built the North Guilford Congregational Church. (THS.)

The interior of the Zion Episcopal Church in a c. 1900 photograph shows the elaborate decoration of the nave, the lanterns for light, and the old organ that church members would take turns pumping with a wooden handle during worship services. On the far right, there is a portion of the gallery and in the upper left-hand corner is a stove pipe. (Zion.)

This photograph of the choir of the Zion Episcopal Church shows what the interior looked liked about 1925. Pictured are, from left to right, ? Bailey, Elizabeth Harrison, Jeanette Colter, Evangeline Stillings, Bill Bailey, Ellsworth Harrison, and Donald Harrison. The pastor is Rev. Francis Smith and the person carrying the cross is Chester Gedney. Note the kerosene lanterns. (Zion.)

This photograph shows Zion Church on its original location on Route 80. Since there was absolutely no room to expand, in 1957 the church was moved to its present site on Notch Hill Road and the parish house added. This is the oldest public building in North Branford. (THS.)

The little St. Augustine's Church on Branford Road was the first Catholic church in town. Built in 1925 on land purchased from Charles Todd, it was a mission church of St. Mary's in Branford and later of St. George's in Guilford. In 1941, eighty-five families in North Branford and sixty-five in Northford were members. The building now houses an insurance company. (St. Augustine's.)

This interior shot of St. Augustine's was taken in 1925, right after the church was built. The church was approximately 35 feet by 50 feet and held about 100 people. With the population explosion after World War II, the church could no longer hold all its communicants, and Mass was held in the junior high school until the new church was built. (Evelyn Surprenant.)

The St. Augustine Rectory was completed in April 1942, and Rev. John J. McCarthy became its first resident pastor. Pictured in front of the rectory is Frances Camarota at the time of her son's wedding, November 17, 1945. (Grace Marx.)

May Procession, the crowning of the Blessed Mother, was a big event at St. Augustine's Church. The Children of Mary, dressed in formal gowns, are shown in front of the old church on May 21, 1946. The teenage girls pictured are, from left to right, Larraine Palluzzi, Aileen Hartigan, Delores Doody, Frances Marrone, Rose Marrone, Peggy Augur, and Lillian Rapone. The little girls are Rosalind Camarota (left), Paula Lupone (center), and Mary Ann Camarota. (Grace Marx.)

The Bare Plain Chapel stood on Route 80 directly across from the Bare Plain Cemetery and was used as a place of religious worship without regard to particular denomination. It was built in 1880 on land donated by Jerome Harrison. Regular services were held with Rev. Charles Page officiating and Isaac Linsley as organist. Funerals were also held here, especially if the deceased had lived some distance away and was being buried in the cemetery. No longer in use, it was abandoned in 1935, later sold, and moved out of town. The land is now the parking lot of the Jerome Harrison School. (Marion Bradley.)

Four

The Schools

Education has always been very important to the people of North Branford. When the Second Society of Branford was established in 1724, one of their first actions was to provide a school for the young, and soon the first schoolhouse was erected near the meetinghouse. The early ministers tutored the older boys, preparing them for further education. Many North Branford and Northford students (a greater proportion than any other Connecticut town) graduated from Yale College.

By 1850 there were seven school districts in town, each with its own one-room schoolhouse, where students received up to an eighth-grade education. When Connecticut advocated the consolidation of the schools in 1918, three new multi-room schools were built during the next eleven years—Center School, the William Douglas School, and the Jerome Harrison School. They served the children of the town until the mid-1950s, when the population explosion resulted in another flurry of school construction.

This photograph of the Totoket School on Mill Road gives a good idea of what the seven one-room schools were like in North Branford. This school was surrounded by open farm fields with the Totoket ridgeline pictured in the distance. (THS.)

The Beech Corner School in District #1 was located at a turn of the road near a grove of beech trees on what is now Beech Street. This photo of the little schoolhouse was taken about 1904. (THS.)

The students and their teacher, Miss Ethel Bent, are shown in front of the Beech Corner School. Among the schoolchildren posing here are seven members of the Harrison family: Jennie Harrison, Emma Harrison (Griswold), Marion Harrison (Rose), Earle Harrison, Leland Harrison, Earle V. Harrison, and Nathan A. Harrison. (THS.)

About 1908, the schoolhouse at Beech Corner was enlarged and the windows moved to the south side. It was used as a school until 1920, when the new Center School was built, but re-opened as a school in the late 1920s when the construction workers at the Lake Gaillard dam moved to town with their families. It later became a dance hall and is now a private residence. (THS.)

These girls, students at the Beech Corner School, posed for a snapshot about 1927. They are, from left to right, as follows: (front row) Dorothy Appell, Marilynn Appell, and Marjorie Bailey; (middle row) three unidentified girls; (back row) Blanche Bailey, two unidentified girls, Emma Snow, and Mary Snow. (THS.)

Center School in District #2 was built in 1876. This building replaced an older schoolhouse that originally stood near the North Branford Congregational Church. It had been moved across Route 80 when the Civil War monument was erected in 1866. In 1920, after the new Center School was built, the building was acquired by the newly formed North Branford Civic Association, which raised funds for community improvements. (THS.)

This 1890 photo shows the teacher and pupils in front of the old Center School. Only two are identified. The girl to the left in the second row is Jennie Rose, who later became a teacher at this school, and the little girl with her arms folded high is Adella Rose. (THS.)

A Center School class photo taken about 1910 shows, from left to right, the following: Reuben Curtis, Ellsworth Foote, Dick Thompson, Francis Todd, Howard Appell, May Holabird, Helen Hegel, Lloyd Harrison, May Lasser, and Fern Stevens. (THS.)

Students pose in front of Center School about 1915. During the 1920s, when it was no longer a school, the Civic Association enlarged the building and added a kitchen wing. They held Saturday night dances that people from surrounding communities often attended. The building, which eventually became known as the Totoket Grange Hall, was also rented to townspeople for large gatherings. Today North Branford Hall is used as a senior center. (THS.)

The District #3 schoolhouse stood on Mill Road. This view shows the east side of the school with its outhouses in the rear. The school was closed in 1929, when the Jerome Harrison School was built. The structure is now a private residence. (THS.)

These girls, students at the Totoket or Mill Road School, posed by a fence in 1921. They are, from left to right, as follows: (front row) Gina Belbusti, Emma Forte, Edith Doolittle, and Marie Hart; (middle row) Mildred Crowe, Marion Jenkins, Laura Amato, and Wanda Ulatowsky; (back row) Liz Rapone, Clara Forte, Eleanor Crowe, Alice Ulatowsky, Frances Spezzano, and Rose Schmidt. (THS.)

A group of Totoket School students are pictured in front of the schoolhouse about 1915. They are, from left to right, as follows: (front row) Rose Spezzano, Edith Cole, and Clarence Hyland; (middle row) Flora Korf, Leta Merrick, Genevieve Page, Bertha Cole, and Viola Schmidt; (top row) Wesley Hyland, Manila Goetz, George Halter, Lucius Merrick, Elbridge Moore, and Carlton Dudley. (Leta Wharton.)

This photograph, taken within a couple of years of the one above, shows many of the same students surrounding their teacher, Etta MacGregor. The students are, from left to right, as follows: (front row) Charles Neubig, Clarence Hyland, and Leta Merrick; (middle row) Beatrice Hyland, Domenic Gidon, Genevieve Page, the teacher, Gladys Cannon, Herbert Neubig, Viola Schmidt, and Bertha Cole; (back row) Lucius Merrick, Carlton Dudley, Flora Corf, Elbridge Moore, Wesley Hyland, Manila Goetz, and Rose Spezzano. (Evelyn Surprenant.)

The District #4 schoolhouse was built in 1805 on Forest Road (Route 22) and is better known today as the Little Red School House. The school served the central geographical area of the town that was and is part of Northford. This photograph, taken about 1890, shows the ten students attending at the time. (THS.)

The old schoolhouse was replaced with this newer building about the turn of the century. Thirty-five students lined up in front of the schoolhouse for this photograph taken in the early 1920s, but unfortunately, they are not identified. When the schools in Northford were consolidated in 1925, the schoolhouse was sold and used as a residence. Now, it is Natureworks, a garden center. (Dorothy Neubig.)

When the newer schoolhouse was built, the 1805 Little Red School House was vacated. For some years it was rented out to farmhands as a residence, but it was later abandoned. In 1928, the building was in a bad state of deterioration, as shown in this photograph, when it was rescued by the League of Women Voters, who moved it to its present location on Old Post Road. (THS.)

The North Branford Chapter of the League of Women Voters, established soon after the women were given the right to vote in 1920, was the first chapter from the League in the United States to be incorporated so it could purchase the 1805 schoolhouse. The restored schoolhouse was used as the Northford Public Library from 1933 to 1957. It is now operated by the Totoket Historical Society as a museum. (THS.)

This October 1912 photograph shows Center School in Northford in District #6. The schoolhouse stood on the site of the present-day William Douglas Commons on Old Post Road. When the new William Douglas School was built in 1925, the old school became the Northford Community House, which was later replaced by a bigger building. The old schoolhouse became the kitchen wing. (THS.)

This photograph shows the interior of the District #6 School in Northford. It was probably taken within a few years of the one above. The students were not identified in either of these two photographs. The Northford Community House, which replaced this school, was moved to its present Clintonville Road site when the additions were constructed at the William Douglas School in 1952. It is now an apartment building. (THS.)

These students attended the District #7 school located on Middletown Avenue west of Reeds Gap Road. In this photograph taken about 1917 or 1918, the children surround their teacher, Miss Gengrande. The students are, from left to right, as follows: (front row) Fiori Bianchi, two unidentified, Fred Bianchi, Delphina Bianchi, and Lawrence Homes; (back row) Herbert C. Miller, Everitt Cooke, Charles L. Miller, and Frank Formisano. (THS.)

Students lined up in front of the District #7 school in 1920, the last year the schoolhouse was used. The building was moved to adjoin a nearby residence, and the students attended the District #6 school in the center of Northford. From left to right are teacher Miss Smith, Merian Burnam, Mary Cavanna, Emil Bianchi, Mary Florence, John Miller, Gerald Florence, Joseph Formisano, August Cavanna, and Fiori Bianchi. (THS.)

The new three-room Center School in North Branford was built in 1920. This photograph was taken when the school was under construction in the spring of 1920. Pictured are, from left to right, Miss Bates, Miss Clough, and an unidentified woman (all teachers), the nurse, and student Clarence Hyland. (THS.)

This is the North Branford Center School Class of 1921. They are, from left to right, as follows: (front row) Eleanor Crowe, Cora Young, Tillie Scholz, Billy Lyons, Anna Leonardo, Florence Daly, Alice Walsh, and Paul Neubig. (middle row) unidentified, Lena Lanza, Nora Walsh, Margarite Bean, Jimmy Lanza, Oscar Schucki, Florence Grovesnor, Elsie Loeber, and Ralph Beers; (back row) Alvin Thompson, Eloise Bean, Ruth Tucker, teacher Miss Clough, Ralph Wigg, Emma Scholz, Mary Camarota, Warren Chidsey, and Jack Forte. (THS.)

70

The entire student body poses in front of Center School in this 1930 photograph. When Cedar Lake School was built in 1960, Center School became the town's first administration building, housing town officials and providing meeting space for the selectmen until the new town hall was built in 1979. Since then, the building has been used by Totoket Historical Society to store its collection and hold its meetings. (THS.)

In 1941, a North Branford Center School class posed for this snapshot. The students are, from left to right, as follows: (front row) unidentified, Agnes Doody, unidentified, Frances Marrone, unidentified, and teacher Rose Alderman; (middle row) unidentified, Paul DaCunto, Rose Marrone, unidentified, Clara Berti, Carol Senecal, Lorraine Wall, and Barbara Juniver; (back row) Edward Amatrudo, Ralph DiPierdomenico, Dennis Hartigan, James Battista, Larraine Palluzzi, Natalie Palluzzi, Roberta Foote, and Peggy Farkash. (THS.)

This 1931 photograph shows the William Douglas School before its additions. Built in 1925, it was named for the town's Revolutionary War hero, Colonel William Douglas, who led the fight against the British on Lake Champlain. The first multi-room school in Northford, it housed the students from four school districts. It was closed in 1982, sold, and renovated as an office building, William Douglas Commons. The students were not identified. (THS.)

This is a William Douglas Class of 1935 portrait. The students are, from left to right, as follows: (front row) Flora Gardner, Frank Marinuzzi, Jean Romberg, William Schanz, Dorothy Huie, Fred Davis, Laura Neif, and Ronald Williams; (middle row) Allan Smith, Walter Palasiewski, Carl Marinuzzi, unidentified, teacher Eleanor Connolly Williams, Rose DelNero, Robert Anderson, Donald Smith, and Emil DelNero; (back row) Bobby Neif, Andrew DeFrancesco, Nicholas Aparia, Teddy Gardner, Frank Savinelli, Mary Swajchuk, Mike Marinuzzi, John Cecarelli, and Pasquale Sanservero. (THS.)

The Jerome Harrison School was built in 1929 on land donated by his nephew, Jonathan Merrick, to be named in his memory. It housed grades one through six, serving the western portion of the town. It later became a junior high school for grades seven and eight. A new school is being built behind it and will open in 1998, replacing the older school. (Louise Mason.)

This is a picture of the 1942 Jerome Harrison graduates from North Branford and Northford. The students are, from left to right, as follows: (front row) Billy Aronson, teacher Olaf Aho, June O'Neill, Marie Rapone, Rose DelNero, Marjorie Boyce, Laura Neff, Alan Bernard, and DeWitt Williams; (middle row) August Rivezzi, Donald Smith, ? Williams, Delia Doolittle, Joyce Bean, Roberta Foote, Antoinette Antigo, ? Newton, Frank Doody, Billy Anderson, and Ward Hill; (back row) Billy Wharton, Robert Colter, Bill Schanz, ? Williams, and Donald Hall. (THS.)

Before the North Branford High School was built in 1964, students from town attended high schools in surrounding communities and New Haven. This photograph shows the North Branford students who entered Guilford High School in 1911, the largest class ever sent from town to any high school up to this time. From left to right are as follows: (seated) Lloyd Dudley Harrison, Richard V. Thompson, and Ellsworth Bishop Foote; (standing) Herbert Rose Harrison, Kenneth Dudley Rose, May Vosburgh Holabird, Marjorie Irma Miller, Irving Nelson Harrison, and Joseph Marks. These students took the Shoreline Trolley to and from school. (THS.)

Five

The Stores, Mills, and Businesses

Although the early settlers in North Branford and Northford were self sufficient, there were items that could not be produced on their farms. Stores have been part of the town since its beginning. At first they were probably located in a room or rooms at one of the houses. In the second half of the nineteenth century, structures were built at each end of town for use as stores. Other stores opened in the twentieth century.

In the early days, sawmills, gristmills, fulling mills, and even linseed "oyl" mills were erected along the rivers in town. During the nineteenth century, manufactories were built between the Farm River and Middletown Turnpike in Northford. They produced a variety of items such as common pins, buttons, hooks and eyes, rivets, horseshoe nails, and tinware. The lack of railroad transportation and the need for greater waterpower caused these factories to move out of town or close. By 1950, there were no mills or factories left. In addition to the factories, there were always small businesses providing specialized services such as shoemaking, tailoring, and blacksmithing.

The store on the corner of Route 80 and North Street was built by Russell Clark in 1851. It replaced an earlier store associated with the Reynolds-Beers House. On the second floor was the Totoket Hall, used for large gatherings, meetings, drama productions, graduations, and dances. In 1909, the store was purchased by Ralph Beers. (THS.)

About 1925, Richard A. Scholz built a small building between the house he owned next to the North Branford cemetery and the Branford River. He operated a store in the front room, and behind the store, there was a pool room where the workers that were building the Water Company dam would come to hang out. (THS—Florence Scholz Hogan.)

In 1928, Scholz purchased the Beers Store from Ralph Beers and continued to run a general store there. The upper floor was converted into an apartment for his large family. He eventually turned the store over to his son Richard, who operated it until 1970. The store was sold several years later, and the building now contains several apartments. (THS.)

During the years that E. Ralph Beers owned the store, it was the town clerk's office. This desk gives evidence that it was a busy place. (THS.)

Mrs. Anna Scholz stands behind the soda fountain in the family store. They also sold meat, groceries, baked goods, and some household products. (THS.)

The Northford Store was built in 1870. The Northford Public Building Association sold 120 shares to raise the $3,000 needed to erect "a suitable building near the Churches for a store, a public hall or halls for town meetings, lectures, singing schools or any other public purposes." The general store was on the ground level, the second floor was a public hall, and the third floor was rented by the Corinthian Lodge #105, a Masonic order. Before this store was built, the store that served Northford residents was located in the old Lorenzo Harrison house on Old Post Road. (THS.)

The Northford Store on Middletown Turnpike had a pot-bellied stove, pickle barrel, and a table for playing cards. Later gas pumps were located out in front. The store was open every day of the week and Sunday until noon. Enlarged into a small supermarket, it is still the Northford Store today. (THS.)

A group gathered in Association Hall on the second floor of the Northford Store sometime in the late nineteenth century. This was the main public hall in this end of town and it was used for community meetings and graduations; during the early years of the twentieth century, it was also the scene of "lively dances." (THS.)

The Bishop house stood on the corner of Route 80 and Notch Hill Road, where a gas station is located today. The small building in the middle of the photograph was the original one-room Center School replaced in 1876 by the larger school building pictured on p. 62. (THS—Elsie Loeber Jones.)

Gus Loeber opened a store in the old Bishop house, as shown in this 1926 photograph. The front rooms of the house were used for the store. This was the way most of the older stores in town were before Russell Clark built a special building for his store in 1851 and the Northford Store was built in 1870. (THS.)

Mrs. Loeber stands behind the counter in Loeber's Store, which sold very much the same kind of goods as the other stores in town. Schoolchildren from Center School sometimes walked to the store for a lunch of vegetable soup and bologna sandwiches or went after school for a soda at the marble soda fountain. (THS.)

Taking advantage of the fact that the Route 80 state highway was a main east-west artery in the state, Loeber's enlarged their store to provide more services. They rented rooms to workers and tourists, and opened a restaurant as well. The store was sold about 1960. (THS.)

Repairing shoes was a trade practiced by some of the farmers as a way of supplementing their income. In a small barn on Quarry Road, an unidentified shoemaker works on shoes for Salvatore Rapone about 1925. The littlest boy in the photograph is Luke Camarota. (THS.)

Cavaliere Forte, who owned the farm on Mill Road, was a butcher trained in the Italian Navy. He came to North Branford to work in the New Haven Trap Rock Commissary. During the 1920s and 1930s he dealt in livestock, meats, groceries, and provisions, making deliveries to New Haven and other area towns. (Henry Forte.)

Amatrudo's gas station was located on Route 80 across from the New Haven Trap Rock Quarry (where Twin Lakes Commons now stands). Michael Amatrudo not only sold gas, but serviced and repaired automobiles in a small garage not shown here. He also sold candy and ice cream. The family house was behind the station, and the house in the photograph belonged to Clare Lanzo, Mrs. Amatrudo's mother. (Linda Cantore.)

This photograph, taken at the end of the nineteenth century, shows the remains of Glover's Grist Mill, located just off Route 80 by Clear Lake Manor Road, near the Guilford line. It gives an indication of what the old mills in town looked like. During the late nineteenth century, George Glover sold agricultural products and animal feeds from this site. (THS.)

The Maltby factory was built about 1850 on the Farm River in Northford. Ax handles, tools, and buttons were manufactured here. Chapman Maltby also made water dippers out of coconut shells, throwing the meat away at first. But experimentation in the Maltby kitchen resulted in a way to dry and preserve the coconut meat. Maltby won first prize at the Philadelphia 1876 Centennial for his shredded (or desiccated) coconut. (THS.)

It was in the Maltby factory that Smith and Cowles manufactured their self-operating horse-drawn hayrake, patented in 1861. Ten years later, David Stevens and his two brothers had a business here printing business cards, and later Christmas, Valentine, and "sparking" cards. They were so successful that twenty-five other printing companies opened factories in town, and Northford became known as the "Christmas card center of the world." (THS.)

This old mill wheel, shown in a photograph taken in 1930, provided the waterpower for the Maltby/Smith/Stevens factory. In the early part of the twentieth century, brushes were made in the old factory building, and it was known as the Brush Shop. The factory was taken down about 1935. (THS.)

This was the dam that provided the waterpower for the Maltby factory and created what was later known as the Brush Shop Pond. The old stone dam was washed out in the flood of 1972. Millpond Tavern was built at the dam site in 1971. (THS.)

The Creamery was located south of the Millpond Tavern on the east side of the Farm River. A thriving business during the later part of the nineteenth and early twentieth centuries, it served the surrounding farms by collecting milk from over three hundred cows. Laborers came down from Vermont and Massachusetts to make cheese and butter that was sold all over the region. (THS.)

This blacksmith shop stood at the intersection of Middletown Avenue and Forest Road (where a gas station is now located). There were several blacksmiths in town. This photograph shows that horses were still being used for transportation in 1927. The boy shown in the picture is Gordon S. Miller, now president of the Totoket Historical Society. (THS.)

This wooden dam was located on the north branch of the Farm River near the Wallingford town line to the east of Woods Hill Road. There was an old sawmill located at this dam. The Totoket Historical Society has in its collection a painting by Wilfred Linsly showing the remains of the old mill. (THS.)

This factory building was located at the "little dam" on the Farm River north of the Northford Manufacturing Company, which stood behind today's Northford Post Office. Owned by Samuel Maltby, the factory produced rivets, hooks, and eyes. The Northford Manufacturing Company was owned by the Bartholomew and Fowler families, and tinware pressed and stamped into useful household goods was manufactured here and shipped all over the country. (THS.)

The dam on Mill Road in North Branford was the site of several mills, the earliest of which were owned by Josiah Darwin, who sold them to the Rogers family in 1754. This 1925 photograph shows the remnants of the sawmill that was located there. On the other side of the dam was Page's Grist Mill. The dam still exists today, creating Page's Pond along the Farm River. (Bertha Page.)

This earlier photograph shows Roger's sawmill in full operation. The sawmill was once owned by the Robinson family. (THS.)

The milk wagon stopped at farms all over town to pick up milk to take to the Creamery. Here it is shown in front of the barn on the Jerome Harrison Farm on Route 80. (Evelyn Surprenant.)

This building, close to the intersection of Route 80 and Totoket Road, was the Totoket Post Office in 1908. It also was one of the card shops in town where cards of various kinds were printed. Today, moved back to its present site, the building is a residence as well as a place of business. (Leta Wharton.)

The Shoreline Trolley ran between New Haven and Guilford from 1911 to 1923 and passed through North Branford, its tracks roughly paralleling Route 80. This photograph shows the trolley station in North Branford that was located on the hill above the Tilcon overpass. The railroad overpass was originally built to span the trolley track. (THS.)

On August 13, 1917, there was a terrible accident on the stretch just west of of the overpass where Commerce Drive is now located. Nineteen people were killed in what was called the worst and most horrible catastrophe in the history of trolleys in New England. The accident was caused when a sleepy motorman did not wait at the switch, resulting in the trolley crashing into another trolley on the track. (THS.)

Six

Industry in the Early Twentieth Century

In 1914, the New Haven Trap Rock Quarry opened its operation on Totoket Mountain and, in doing so, began a new era in North Branford. It was the first large-scale industry in town, and many men from other places came to work at the quarry, bringing their families with them.

Ten years later, the New Haven Water Company started to acquire land in the valley surrounded on three sides by Totoket Mountain, and it eventually built the huge dam that created the second largest lake in Connecticut. These two events, in the first quarter of the twentieth century, impacted the geography, population, and demographics of the town.

With the population explosion that occurred after World War II, North Branford was changed forever from a small quiet rural town to the suburban community it is today.

The Hart brothers, John and Alex, operate the steam shovel at the quarry in this 1914 photograph taken soon after the trap rock quarry opened. The railroad cars would be loaded to carry the chunks of rock to the crusher and screening house. Note the horse and wagon on top of the hill above the quarry face. (Ellen Spencer.)

Joe Camarota, one of the quarry's first foremen, operates the steam engine at the New Haven Trap Rock Quarry in 1914. The name "trap rock" comes from the German word *treppen*, meaning steps. The basalt rock quarried here for bituminous concrete containing asphalt and stone, road bases, and rip-rap banks is angular and breaks in such a way as to form steps. (THS.)

This panoramic view of the newly opened New Haven Trap Rock Quarry on the Totoket ridge shows the short length of the quarry face in 1914. Later it became the longest, single-faced quarry in the world. The train on the upper track would transport the stone from the quarry face

This view shows the crusher and screening house at the Trap Rock Quarry about 1920. The crushed trap rock would travel by conveyor to the building on the right where it would be sorted and loaded on the railroad cars that transported it via the Branford Steam Railway to barges at the docks in Pine Orchard. From there, it was shipped all over the East Coast. (THS.)

to the crusher. A second set of tracks in front of the crusher would carry the processed rock to the docks in Branford. (THS.)

A Y-shaped tunnel was built into the face of the quarry for the blast. This photograph shows the entrance to the tunnel into the mountain. Boxes of dynamite would be placed in the entire tunnel, wired to a fuse, and then, at a safe distance, wired to the detonator. During World War II, Salvatore Rapone was in charge of the blasting and built this tunnel. (THS.)

This photograph was taken the exact time of a blast. You can see the pieces of rock suspended in mid-air in the center of the photograph. The reason the photograph is blurry is that the force of the blast not only shook the ground but the photographer, Joseph Buccelli, as well. (THS.)

Enormous piles of rock were left in the aftermath of the blast. This photograph and the previous two on p. 94 were all taken on the same day in the mid-1940s. Blasting was done three or four times a year prior to 1950. The whistle would blow a twenty-minute warning so nearby residents could safeguard fragile items in their houses before the blast would shake the earth. (THS.)

At the time this photograph was taken, about thirty years after the quarry began its operation, enormous trucks replaced the railroad cars conveying the rock blasted from the quarry face to the crusher. Superintendent Edward Wall Sr. (right) shows off the quarry operation to a sales representative, Mr. Penn. (THS.)

James McKeown Sr. (1902–1973) worked at the Trap Rock Quarry as a brakeman on the railroad in 1927. Single at the time, he boarded at Strickland's house on Mill Road. Other workers boarded at other homes in North Branford or lived dormitory style at the Commissary, owned by the company on the quarry property. (James McKeown Jr.)

Engine #2 of the Branford Steam Railroad carried trap rock from the quarry to the docks at Pine Orchard in Branford. Pictured are engineer Daniel Marroney, who worked at the quarry for sixty years, and brakeman Salvatore Rapone during the mid-1940s. (THS.)

Engine #27 was used within the quarry to transport stone from the quarry face to the crusher. This engine had been used to rebuild the Branford Steam Railroad, originally built by Louis Fisk to transport people to the horse racing track at Damascus in Branford. The little engine, according to Bill Clossom, ran very quietly and emitted a long plume of white smoke, unlike the noisy and smoky #41. (THS.)

Gardner Hughes was an electrician working at the quarry from 1918 to 1963. The quarry had electricity long before the rest of North Branford. Hughes moved to town to work at the quarry and lived in one of five houses owned by the company. Three of the houses are still standing on Quarry Road. He is pictured here on top of the quarry near the huge Euclid trucks. (THS.)

The land in the quiet farm valley that lay between the Totoket Mountain ridge and Sea Hill was acquired in the mid-1920s by the New Haven Water Company. This is the east half of the basin. Over thirty homes, farms, and other buildings in the valley were demolished to make room for a reservoir that is part of a system that stretches from Madison to New Haven. (THS.)

In the spring of 1926, work began on the North Branford dam. It is 1,200 feet long, 100 feet high, 11 feet wide at the top, and 85 feet wide at the base. The excavation for the dam was 70 feet deep. This photograph was taken on June 1, 1926. (THS.)

By April 28, 1927, the huge dam had begun to take shape. It was built in sections to allow for shrinkage during cold weather. Slip joints prevent the water from coming through. The house in the background had been owned by the Allen family and was used as the superintendent's office during the dam's construction. (THS.)

A year later, on July 1, 1927, the Totoket dam was nearing completion. (THS.)

This is one of the houses that stood in the valley and had to be removed. The house, belonging to Nathan Harrison, had been built not long before the land was acquired for the reservoir. It was moved to a site on what is now Beech Street and still stands today. (THS.)

This lovely house was taken down to make way for the dam. It belonged to John Harrison, a descendent of one of the town's earliest settlers. The Harrisons—John, Royal, and Albert—owned a great deal of land in the valley. (THS.)

The Rose-Curtis House, one of the oldest houses in town, was built in 1724 by Jonathan Rose and sold about 1882 by his descendants to Rev. William Curtis. This house was demolished, but two of the rooms were preserved and reassembled in the Yale University Art Gallery. They are called the Branford Rooms. The Totoket Historical Society owns a miniature model replica of one of the rooms. (THS.)

The barn complex on the Albert Harrison Farm also disappeared under the lake. When the water in the lake is low, remnants of the foundations of some of the buildings can be seen. (THS.)

The valley began to flood after the dam was complete in 1928. The Allen house, used for the superintendent's office, is beginning to be surrounded by water. It took four years to flood the entire valley and create Lake Gaillard. (THS.)

The Cole house was saved, moved, and used as a boathouse. In early years the dam was open to the public, but since 1968, it has been closed and only opened for specific events such as the recreation department's bike-hikes or the North Branford Congregational Church-sponsored Ecumenical Easter Sunrise Service. The Regional Water Company is planning to open it sometime in the future for hiking by permit. (THS.)

Seven

At Their Leisure

Life was more difficult during the years from 1850 to 1950 without the labor-saving devices we enjoy today. Men worked long hours on the farms or at the quarry making a living for their families. Women, too, worked hard, orchestrating life at home and sometimes earning their own living. However, the families of North Branford and Northford set aside time to participate in church and school activities, civic organizations and clubs, and various sports and other leisure activities.

There were special occasions, like celebrations, fairs, carnivals, and parades. Organizations would hold dances, plays, and shows to raise money for community services, which also provided opportunities to socialize and enjoy one anothers' company. The photographs in this chapter show some of the ways in which the townspeople filled their leisure hours.

Students from the Totoket School on Mill Road travel in Grandpa Wilbor Hyland's truck to a school picnic at the Goodrich cottage at lower Indian Point in Branford about 1919. (THS.)

The North Branford Fair was held in 1885. Here rows of oxen line up for judging in the farm fields located between Notch Hill Road (Route 22) and Branford Road (Route 139) just southeast of the village center. (THS.)

In October 1908, the Totoket Grange #83 entered a float at the Branford Carnival held on the Branford Green. Stephen Rose helped trim the float, and the horse team belonged to William Carey, the driver. Seated on the float are Miss Ethel Bent (a teacher at the Beech Corner School), Ethel Fowler, and Olive Rose. (THS.)

Lucy Holabird and Ethel Bergstresser decorated their trap pulled by their horse, Frank, and rode in the parade at the Branford Carnival in 1912. (THS.)

This photograph shows a school float from North Branford at the Guilford Fair, *c.* 1915. (THS.)

These students at the North Branford Center School, costumed for a school play about 1910, are, from left to right, as follows: (boys) Herbert Harrison, Leland Harrison, unidentified, Nathan Harrison, Irving Harrison, Lloyd Harrison, Robert Cole, Kenneth Rose, Ellsworth Foote, and Fred Harrison; (girls) May Holabird, Effie Holabird, Helen Hegel, Fern Stevens, Jennie Harrison, Rosalie Appell, Isabel Harrison, Hazel Stevens, Marjorie Miller, and Marion Harrison. (THS.)

Local residents became actors and actresses in a Biblical play, *The Rock*, put on by the North Branford Congregational Church at the North Branford Hall about 1930. Pictured are, from left to right, Orrin Snow, Phyllis Holabird, Patrick Walsh, Mary Snow, Rev. Teague Hipps, May Holabird, Vernon Gedney, Jeanette Hill, and Russell Holabird. (NBCC.)

All the students from the North Branford Center School were involved in a production of *Hanzel and Gretel* at North Branford Hall, *c.* 1939. The students either performed in the play, sang in the chorus, or played an instrument in the orchestra. (THS—Paul Boyce Collection.)

The Totoket Grange #83 put on minstrel shows during the late 1940s. They are, from left to right, as follows: (front row) Leslie Brindley, Elsie Frawley, John Wittmer, Arthur Maynard, Ed Wall, Frank Hazlett, Burton Hall, and May Wittmer; (second row) Edward Donadio, Bernie Amatrudo, Donald Frawley, unidentified, Ethel Brindley, Mary Donadio, and Tom Bernard; (third row) Burt Colter, Roberta Hawkins, Natalie Oboyski, Margaret Vogt, Clarice Davis, Lilian Rapone, Mary Hawkins, Cynthia Wall, Muriel Appell, Jeanette Colter, and Alice Brindley; (back row) Tom Colter, Dennis Hartigan, Ed Wall Jr., Mary Bernard, Edward Amatrudo, unidentified, Jerry Wall, Alfred Hawkins, and John Adamoli. (THS.)

These gentlemen, members of an unknown organization or club, posed for a formal photograph about 1870. They are George Babcock, David Stent, Isaac Linsley, David Rose, Herbert Page, Preston Linsley, Newton Robinson, R. Clark Russell, John Rose, and Frank Gates. (Bertha Page.)

Ladies of the Idle Hour Club gathered for a photograph, c. 1930. The Idle Hour Club was formed when a group of women in North Branford decided to get together and do nothing for one hour, just be together and socialize. (Leta Wharton.)

May and Elbertine Merrick gave a party for their friends in 1914. Note that all the guests wore hats. (Evelyn Surprenant.)

The Ladies Sewing Society poses on the chapel steps about 1922. The women are, from left to right, as follows: (seated, first row) Marion Reed Hartigan (with son John), Vincent Griswold, Pauline Harrison (with two children), and Carleton Harrison; (second row) Ruth Beers, Emma Griswold, and Lucy Holabird; (third row) Leila Holabird, unidentified, Hazel Hill, Mrs. Nathan Rose, and Sally Rose; (standing) Mary Fowler, Anna Leonard, Mrs. Whealdon, Mrs. Roy Harrison, and Mrs. Fred Stevens; (top of steps) Beatrice Hyland, Miriam Rose, Nellie Chidsey, Florence Andrews, Addie Rose, an unidentified woman, and Mabel Bartholomew. (NBCC.)

This is the North Branford Fife and Drum Corps. They are, from left to right, as follows: (front row) George Appell, Bud Scholz, Luke Camarota, Tony Rivezzi, Ralph Colter, Anthony Daly, John Farkash, Bernard Strickland, John Mickmac, Forrest Hill, Arnold Schloeman, Ed Linsley, Raymond O'Brien, Vincent Griswold, Thomas Walsh, Louis Marrone, John Hartigan Jr., Nick Buccelli Jr., Charles Linsley, and Henry Strickland; (back row) Ralph Helen, Albert Harrison, Joe Marrone, Anthony Camarota, Sally Buccelli, Andrew DaCunto, Edwin Strickland, Domenic Marrone, unidentified, Joe Buccelli, Jerry Buccelli, Armand Provanzano, and two unidentified. (THS.)

The Fife and Drum Corps was organized in 1933 by Earl Colter Sr. as an activity for the young boys in town. Here the Corps performs during the Memorial Day services on the North Branford Green sometime before World War II. The Corps has been a fixture in Memorial Day parades and ceremonies from the time it was organized. (THS.)

The Fife and Drum Corps is still going strong today with some of its original members. This 1943 photograph shows a very depleted group because most of those young boys shown in the photograph on the previous page were in the various branches of service. (THS.)

Corps members and their supporters relax in the Clubhouse about 1940. They are, from left to right, as follows: (front row) Joe Marrone, Ralph Marrone, unidentified, Sally Buccelli, and Earl Colter Sr.; (second row) unidentified, Robert Colter, Ralph Colter, Andrew DaCunto, John Hartigan Jr., Frank Hazlett, and Alex McKernan; (third row) Louis Marrone, two unidentified, and Henry Forte; (back row) Eddie Rubendunce, Andrew Amatrudo, unidentified, Alex Paluzzi, Dennis Hartigan, Frank Whitney, Paul DaCunto Jr., and Eddie Amatrudo. (THS.)

After decorating the graves in the cemeteries and marching in the parade, the schoolchildren in town would gather on the Green to participate in the Memorial Day ceremonies. The program would be a lengthy one with speeches, recitations, and songs. Here on May 30, 1936, one of the ministers in town addresses the audience. (THS.)

On Memorial Day, 1938, the fifth-grade students give a presentation. The students and residents of Northford had their own parade and ceremonies to celebrate Memorial Day. Today Memorial Day is still celebrated by a parade and short ceremony, but the location alternates each year between the ends of town. (THS.)

A Boy Scout troop marches by Loeber's Store in the 1941 North Branford Memorial Day parade. (THS.)

The Red Cross Corps, led by Katherine Richmond (left), Billie Schuessler (center), and Alice Brindley, marches in the 1944 Memorial Day Parade. At that time the parade assembled at the Clubhouse, marched east on Route 80, around the triangle shaped by the forked intersection at Sea Hill Road, and retraced their route back to the Green at the North Branford Congregational Church. (THS.)

The 1935 Connecticut Tercentenary was an occasion of celebrations at both ends of town. Northford held a parade along Middletown Turnpike, a band concert and luncheon at the Community House, and a historical pageant at the Northford Congregational Church. Here Helen Walsh Augur (far left), George H. Augur (center left), Grace Augur Neubig (center right), and Ida Augur (far right) are appropriately dressed for the occasion. (Ann Neubig.)

North Branford celebrated the weekend of July 27 and 28, 1935. On Saturday there was a parade, exhibition drills by several fife and drum corps, a hobby show, luncheon, baseball game, historical pageant, and street dance. On Sunday, tercentenary commemorative services were held in the churches and the hobby show at the town hall. This photograph shows the float of the Ladies Sewing Society, which portrays the homemade crafts of yesteryear. (THS.)

In the North Branford Tercentenary Parade, Chester Gedney goes West in an old Conestoga wagon. (THS.)

This photograph shows the Totoket Grange #83 float in the North Branford Tercentenary Parade with Ernest Linsley, Frank Mackey, Barbara Juniver, and Charles Linsley. This photograph was taken on Branford Road (Route 139) where the Fleet Bank is now located. Totoket Grange #83 is still a viable organization today, meeting once a month and participating in community activities and service. (THS.)

During the coldest months, the mill ponds along the Farm River would freeze up, and on Sundays, Northford residents would enjoy an afternoon of ice skating. About 1918, Martin Trieschmann and a couple of friends took a break from their hockey game to pose for this snapshot at the Big Pond. (Gertrude Heath.)

In 1930, North Branford had a football team. They are, from left to right, as follows: (front row) Kenny Bunnell, James Lanzo, Thomas Walsh, George Chasney, Joe DeSantis, and Burton Colter Jr.; (second row) Burt Colter Sr., Charlie Bauer, Leslie Bean, Steven DeSantis, Joe Munson, John Darling, unidentified, and James Walsh; (back row) John Walsh, unidentified, Joe Grasso, Orlando ?, Ed Wall Sr., Earl Colter Jr., unidentified, Bill Ahearn, ? Fitzgerald, and Jack Wall. (THS.)

Organized sports became very popular during the twentieth century. The 1931–32 junior basketball team was the town and county champions. They are, from left to right, as follows: (front row) John Darling, Earl Colter Jr., Russell Holabird, and Patrick Walsh; (back row) Steve DeSantis, Bill Wall, Rev. Dillard Lessley of the North Branford Congregational Church, Burton Colter Jr., and Leslie Bean. (THS.)

The 1931 senior basketball team is shown in this photograph. They are, from left to right, as follows: (front row) John Walsh, Mugsy Parsinski, Carlie Stevens, Ed Wall Sr., and Whitey Fair; (back row) Burt Colter Jr., ? Morse, Jimmy Walsh, Pat Walsh, and Kenny Bunnell. The Clubhouse, shown in the background of the Fife and Drum Corps photograph on p. 110 and located where McDonald's is today, was originally the North Branford Athletic Club. (THS.)

Along the Branford River just off Valley Road was a stretch of river where only women could fish. The cabin shown here was the Women's Rest House, located there until the 1970s. It was also known as the Ladies' Fishing Cabin. (THS.)

In this photograph a lady fisherman tries her luck along the Farm River in Northford by the Augur Road bridge. (Gertrude Heath.)

Allen (left), Emory (center), and Bill Meyerjack play with a calf at the Shagbark Dairy Farm on Old Turnpike Road during the summer of 1942. (Barbara Stone.)

Clifford Harrison poses with his owls at the Harrison family farm, which was located in the valley taken over by the New Haven Water Company. This was a rare sight in 1915 and would probably would not be seen today. (Dudley Harrison.)

Horse racing was a popular pastime in town for hundreds of years. Here a Sunday horse race and show takes place on the Trieschmanm Farm in Northford about 1900. (Gertrude Heath.)

Schoolchildren participate in field day activities in the field next to the Zion Church. North Branford Town Hall is now located on this spot. Schoolchildren still enjoy field day activities at the various schools in town. (THS.)

In Northford, the Shipman Athletic Field was located north of the present Northford Post Office. It was used for many years early in the twentieth century for athletics and outings. Here a group of unidentified women pose under the Shipman Field flag. The only other playing field in town until 1950 was the baseball field at the Clubhouse on land that is now the Central Shopping Plaza. (Gertrude Heath.)

Just hanging around and playing boccie at the Clubhouse about 1949 are, from left to right, Fiore Rapone, Ed Wall Sr., Sal Rapone, and Bruno DiNardi. (Grace Marx.)

In addition to their more serious duties, the volunteer fire companies in both ends of town have been involved in many social activities. This photograph taken a couple of years after the North Branford Volunteer Fire Department was established in 1938, shows not only the members of Company #1, but the town constables and some members of the Fife and Drum Corps. Holding the flag is John Hartigan and an unidentified person. The other people in the photograph, from left to right, are as follows: (front row) Charlie Leonard, unidentified, Nate Harrison, Leslie Brindley, Chester Gedney, unidentified, Burt Colter Jr., Tom Colter, Paul Boyce, unidentified, Mike Amatrudo, two unidentified persons, and Paul DaCunto Sr; (back row) Domenic Marrone, Anthony Daly, Luke Camarota, Joe Marrone, Tony Rapone, Tony DaCunto, unidentified, and Rev. Lessley. The first firehouse was in Nate Harrison's garage on North Street. It served as North Branford's firehouse until the new one was built on Route 80 in the 1950s. (THS.)

A meeting of the board of fire commissioners was held at the Company #2 Firehouse in Northford about 1947. Company #2 was formed in 1945, and a firehouse was built in the same location where the firehouse is today. The people in this picture are, from left to right, as follows: (seated) Mike Amatrudo, Bob Newton, John Hartigan, Leslie Brindley, and Nate Harrison; (standing) ? Augur, Chester Gedney, unidentified, Edward Russell, and unidentified. (THS.)

On Memorial Day in 1939, the members of the Volunteer Fire Department parade by the old Training Ground where the Atwater Library now stands. Firemen, their fire engines, and the Ladies Auxiliaries have been part of the parade every year since the fire department was founded in 1938. Those identified are, from left to right, as follows: John Hartigan, Paul Boyce, Leslie Brindley, Chester Gedney, and Mike Amatrudo. (THS.)

The Charles Atwater Memorial Library was built in 1942 on the Old Training Ground, or "Little Green," which was used for militia training from 1765 to the Civil War. The library was built with funds donated by the descendants of Rev. Charles Atwater, the third minister of the North Branford Congregational Church, in his memory. (THS—Paul Boyce Collection.)

This shot shows the interior of the Atwater Library soon after it opened. The clock belonged to the Atwater family. Additions to both town libraries during the 1960s have changed the appearance of the original library buildings. (THS—Paul Boyce Collection.)

City Mission Camp was located on a hill south of Route 80 just past the town center. This photo taken from Sea Hill Road about 1940 shows the camp in the distance. Underprivileged children from New Haven would spend a week or two here during the summer. The camp closed in the 1950s, and the hill was removed to provide fill for the interstate highway construction. (THS—Paul Boyce Collection.)

The Polish Roman Catholic Union Picnic Pavilion was located north of Route 80 on Totoket Road. The union held dances every Sunday during the 1940s, and the pavilion was rented for large gatherings during warm weather. The building is now gone, and a small industrial park is located on its site. (THS.)

Veterans of World War II posed for this picture after a dinner given for them at the Polish Hall by grateful residents in 1946. They are, from left to right, as follows: (front row) Merwin Appell, Armand Provanzano, Tony DaCunto, brothers Joe, Domenic, Louis, and Ralph Marrone, Burt Colter Jr., Andrew DaCunto, John Farkash, Jud Page, and Frank Velush; (second row) unidentified, Emerson Surprenant, Peter Grossi, Shirley Harrison, Marie Hart, Elsie Forte, unidentified, Waldo Hogan, Al Harrison, Bud Hill, Paul Hill, and Augie Querfeld; (third row)

unidentified, Victor Panko, Ed Krista, Ralph Colter, David Burr, Forrest Hill, Frank Doody, Olaf Aho, unidentified, Vincent Griswold, two unidentified persons, and Whitey Fair; (fourth row) Earl Colter, George Hall, Irving Hall, Joe Camarota, Ralph Haley, Anthony Daly, unidentified, John Hartigan, unidentified, Al Caputo, Al Rothkowski, and Al Hart; (back row) Tom Fowler, Charles Linsley, Ed Linsley, Ray Bahnsen, Anthony Camarota, unidentified, George Appell, brothers Edward, Charles, Steve, and Bernard Strickland.

Three firemen stop to view the World War II Honor Roll on the Green after Memorial Day exercises in 1944. The Honor Roll listed the men and women who served and were serving in the war. (THS.)

North Branford and Northford changed after World War II. No longer will you see a horse and sleigh gliding down a quiet country road on a cold winter afternoon. Here Alta Ross and her husband take a Sunday ride down North Street in January 1939. (Dudley Harrison.)